Romeo and Juliet

For Kids

by
Lois Burdett

FIREFLY BOOKS

A FIREFLY BOOK

Published by Firefly Books Ltd.
Copyright © 1998 Lois Burdett
Third printing, 2004

Library of Congress Cataloguing-in-Publication Data available.

Canadian Cataloguing in Publication Data

Burdett, Lois
  Romeo and Juliet for Kids

(Shakespeare can be fun)
ISBN 1-55209-244-5 (bound) ISBN 1-55209-229-1 (pbk.)

1. Children's plays, Canadian (English).* 2. Children's poetry, Canadian (English).* 3. Readers' theatre.
I. Shakespeare, William, 1564–1616. Romeo and Juliet
II. Title. III. Series.

PR2878.R65B87 1998   jC812'.54   C98-930369-1

Published in Canada by
Firefly Books Ltd.
66 Leek Crescent
Richmond Hill, Ontario
L4B 1H1

Published in the United States by
Firefly Books (U.S.) Inc.
P.O. Box 1338, Ellicott Station
Buffalo, New York 14205

Printed and bound in Canada
by Friesens, Altona, Manitoba

Design concept by Lois Burdett
Design production by Fortunato Design Inc.

Canadä

The Publisher acknowledges the financial support of the Government of Canada through the Book Publishing Industry Development Program for our publishing activities.

Other books in the series:
A Child's Portrait of Shakespeare
Twelfth Night for Kids
Macbeth for Kids
A Midsummer Night's Dream for Kids
The Tempest for Kids

Robin Wilhelm

Lois Burdett's Grades 2 and 3 class

Foreword

I have long been a fan of Lois Burdett and her ever-changing troupe of student players. As a former member of the Stratford Festival Company, I have had the good fortune to witness many of their performances, both at the school and on the Festival stage. I have never left one of their shows unmoved. The passion, the delight, and – most remarkably – the simplicity in their playing of Shakespeare is a humbling reminder that the most important thing is "to tell the story." And once we discard old notions of how these stories should be told, we're ready to treat Shakespeare as an ally and not an alien spouting a language we can't hope to comprehend.

Lois's success should encourage all those who want to challenge young people and plant the seeds for a lifelong relationship with a playwright whose work repays any study tenfold. Her simplified versions of the plays manage to retain most of the poetry and all of the wonder of the originals. *Romeo and Juliet for Kids*, the latest in this terrific series, is no exception. I know the play pretty well, having done it twice at Stratford – first as Romeo, then as Mercutio. So I'm very confident in my claim.

Like riding a bike, once children learn to engage their imagination they'll never forget how, but will use it as a tool to take them to a place they've never been: the future. One of my favourite theatre teachers once said that if you could do Shakespeare you could do anything, and I believe him. Yes, it takes some time and care to learn to read his clues and explore his mysteries, but that's what a lifetime is for. One of the saddest things I have ever heard in a theatre is, "Well, it's Shakespeare. I'm not meant to understand it." Rubbish! Shakespeare wrote for audiences who were largely illiterate. They couldn't stop a performance to study a text, but they might very well have hurled a half-eaten sausage at you if you failed to be clear and simple. Lois understands this perfectly. She has found a way to blow the dust off "Old Bill" and let her students revel in their understanding. Their enthusiasm for sharing Shakespeare's stories is overwhelming.

I am a firm believer in starting things early. Reading aloud to my own children has convinced me that the sooner you spark their interest, the better. From Gertrude and Hamlet to Green Eggs and Ham, they soak it all in like water in sand. It is my fondest hope that Lois's books will be dog-eared and thumbed by large hands and small, and that her success will encourage parents and teachers everywhere. There is nothing so gratifying as those three small words that say it all, "Again, Daddy, again!"

COLM FEORE, *Father-Actor*

THE CHARACTERS

The Court

PRINCE ESCALUS . . . . Prince of Verona

COUNT PARIS ⎫

MERCUTIO ⎭ . . . . Kinsmen of the Prince

The House of Capulet

JULIET . . . . Daughter of the Capulets

LORD CAPULET . . . . Juliet's father

LADY CAPULET . . . . Juliet's mother

TYBALT . . . . Juliet's friend and cousin

NURSE . . . . Juliet's servant

PETER . . . . Capulet's servant

PARTY GUESTS . . . . Invited by the Capulets

The House of Montague

ROMEO . . . . Son of the Montagues

LORD MONTAGUE . . . . Romeo's father

LADY MONTAGUE . . . . Romeo's mother

BENVOLIO . . . . Romeo's friend and cousin

BALTHASAR . . . . Romeo's servant

PARTY MASQUERS . . . . Not invited by the Capulets

Others

FRIAR LAURENCE . . . . A monk

FRIAR JOHN . . . . Another monk

APOTHECARY . . . . A druggist

AND

MONTAGUE'S SERVANTS

CAPULET'S SERVANTS

CITIZENS OF VERONA

Dion Lach
(age 8)

I have a story from another age,
A tale of resentment and bitter rage.
In fair Verona, where I set my scene,
Violent brawls had become routine.
Two noble families were locked in this fight,
Hatred burned in their souls; they could never unite.
One was called Capulet, the other Montague,
And neither household would change its view.

No one remembers the cause of their feud,
But all were affected by its angry mood.
Each Montague and Capulet child and relation
Passed on this quarrel to the next generation.
Even the servants were spiteful and mean,
And Verona had become far from serene.
Twice that summer in the sweltering heat,
The Capulets and Montagues fought in the street.

Anika Johnson (age 8)

And now once again tempers flared
As a new argument was declared.
Two Capulet servants taunted Montague's men,
Swords were drawn, and they were at it again.
There were smashing blows; each side was skilled.
Blood boiled, begging to be spilled.
A young man, Benvolio, plunged into the fray,
"Part, fools!" he shouted, in a worried way.
"Put up your swords. You know not what you do!"
For he was a gentleman, yet a Montague too.

Benvolio

Fire gloomed in their eyes. They didn't even look at each other for their last names were Montague and Capulet. Swords whizzed through the air with a swish and a swash. There was a great clashing of blades and the fight raged on.

Story: Piers Fox (age 7)
Picture: Alex Fitzpatrick (age 7)

But Tybalt, a Capulet, who welcomed a scrap,
Stormed into the group like a thunderclap.
"Turn thee, Benvolio, look upon thy death.
I will hate the word Montague to my last breath!"
Within seconds, the market place was aroar,
As Verona's citizens joined by the score.
Even old Capulet and old Montague
Drew their swords high to reap their due.
And so as you see, from one small threat
A battle began that no one would forget.

Tybalt

Dear Grandmother,
It's your granddaughter Alice here. We think you'd better not come to visit. Verona isn't as peaceful as it seems. The MONTAGUES and the CAPULETS are in action again. Today there was a massive fight in the street. I don't even know which side to cheer for. All the shouting has given me a dreadful headache!!
Alice

Story: Courtney Vandersleen (age 7)
Picture: Sydney Truelove (age 7)

Then trumpets hailed the mighty Prince,
Making both families cower and wince.
Prince Escalus declared, "This violence must cease.
Rebellious subjects, enemies to peace."
His face was severe as he looked around,
"Throw your mistempered weapons to the ground!
And if ever again you go astray,
Be it known now, with your lives you will pay.
You, Capulet, shall come along with me.
And, Montague, this afternoon I will see.
I demand from you both, a change of heart.
Once more, on pain of death, all men depart!"

Lord Capulet

Lord Montague

Prince Escalus

Eliza Johnson (age 8)

But one young lad had stayed away,
And did not brandish a sword that day.
Romeo Montague was his name,
A nobleman of great wealth and fame.
He sat alone in his chamber room,
And moped about in a state of gloom.
He shut up his windows and locked out the light,
And made himself an artificial night.
This mood was hard for his parents to endure.
Benvolio, his friend, told them he'd find a cure.
"See where he comes. So please you step aside,
I'll know his grievance or be much denied.
Good morrow, cousin. What trouble overpowers?
What sadness lengthens Romeo's hours?"

Romeo

Dear Benvolio,
What am I to do to get Romeo to reveal his pain? I would give quite anything to hear what is the cure for my sorrow stricken son. The truth stays jammed in his heart.
            Lady Montague

Story: Ellen Stuart (age 8)
Picture: Dulcie Vousden (age 9)

10

It didn't take long to ascertain
The cause of Romeo's heartache and pain.
He was devoted to a lady divine,
A beautiful woman called Rosaline.
The love he craved, she had denied.
"It's all very clear," Romeo sighed,
"She hath forsworn to love, and in that vow
Do I live dead that live to tell it now."
Benvolio cautioned, "Don't be so blind!
Banish this female from your mind!
Take my advice and do not despair.
Examine other beauties and compare!"
Romeo moaned, "I'll remember her still.
I love Rosaline, and I always will!"

Story: Ellen Stuart (age 8)
Picture: Megan Vandersleen (age 9)

While the Montague family continued to brood,
The Capulets were in a festive mood.
Even the servants were feeling hearty,
As they bustled about arranging a party.
Just then a young man entered the hall.
It was Count Paris, who had come to call.
Paris bowed low in a manner grand,
"I'm here to ask for your daughter's hand."
Lord Capulet replied, "She's not yet fourteen,
But, good Paris, I'll let you intervene.
My will to her consent is but a part.
It is up to you to win her heart.
I'm having a party this very night.
You are invited to dance and delight!"

Lord Capulet, please let me marry Juliet. She is the one I foresee with me. Thirteen is not that young. My dad married my mom at that age. It's not the years that are important! It's the love and there's a lot of love in this case. Wake up good man. It's the 1590's!

Paris

Count Paris

David Marklevitz (age 8)

Ashley Kropf (age 10)

Capulet called to his servant, "Hasten through town,
Invite those people whose names I've written down."
Peter intended to do the deed,
But there was a problem. He couldn't read!
When he met Romeo, he asked him to assist,
"Please, Sir! Can you read the words on this list?"
Romeo obliged and announced every name:
"A noble company of fortune and fame!"
The servant told Romeo, "You can come too!
If you be not of the house of Montague!"
Benvolio urged, "My friend, if you dare,
We'll go to the dance. Rosaline will be there!
Compare her face with some that I shall show,
And I will make thee think thy swan a crow."

Peter

I have an awful problem! I can't read a word on this list, not a peep of a word. I need help and quick or I'll be fired !!!
Peter

Story: Josh Strasler (age 7)
Picture: Ashley Kropf (age 10)

Back at the Capulets, there was quite a fuss.
Juliet's mother had something to discuss.
"Tell me daughter, would you like to marry?"
Juliet was shocked; her voice grew wary,
"It is an honour that I dream not of!"
But her mother continued to talk of love.
"The valiant Paris seeks you for his wife.
His charms and wealth will enhance your life.
I advise you to give him a chance at least.
Observe his appearance tonight at the feast."
The nurse joined in with more words of praise,
"Go, girl, seek happy nights to happy days."

Lady Capulet

My sweet Juliet,
The gallant Paris seeks
your hand in marriage.
The two of you would
make a charming match.
Now what do you say to
that my dear daughter?
Tonight at the grand ball
we are hosting you will
meet the fine youth.
You won't be disappointed.
          Lady Capulet

Story: Brock Wreford (age 7)
Picture: Kate Vanstone (age 10)

14

Later that evening, torches flared bright.
Romeo met his friends in the flickering light.
They were all dressed in fanciful disguise,
And held gilded masks to cover their eyes.
But Romeo was still suffering from the blues,
"Mercutio, my friend, you have dancing shoes!
I'm not like you. I have a soul of lead.
Give me a torch. I will bear the light instead."
Mercutio chided, "Where's your romance?
Borrow Cupid's wings. We must have you dance!"
Benvolio added, "Hurry up, we'll be late!"
"I fear too early!" Romeo pondered his fate.
"These revels tonight," he said under his breath,
"Begin the grim march to my untimely death."

Oh Romeo, get a life! The dance will be the perfect medicine for you! You're a downright party pooper in my point of view. You'll spoil it if you keep up this "oh I can't go" attitude of yours. Come on Romeo, let's PARTY!!!
Mercutio

Story and picture: Anika Johnson (age 8)

Old Capulet greeted them in the great hall,
"Welcome, my friends, one and all!
Join the party!" he said with a grin,
"Come musicians, let the mirth begin."
In a matter of moments the room was aglow,
The ladies and gentlemen danced to and fro.
But Romeo stood by himself at the side
Until, in an instant, his eyes opened wide.
He gazed on a vision he'd never forget.
Across the room was the fair Juliet.
Now Rosaline's beauty lost its glow,
"What lady's that?" asked Romeo.
"Oh, she doth teach the torches to burn bright,
For I ne'er saw true beauty till this night!"

Juliet

I have seen the woman of my dreams. Not only is she a swan this girl is a dove! Thoughts of Rosaline vanished into the forgotten mist of my mind. My cheeks blushed pink. My eyes grew as big as saucers. My heart was on fire! Oh my lady if only I knew your name.

Romeo

Story: Sean McGarry (age 7)
Picture: Caitlin More (age 9)

His words were heard by a Capulet nearby.
Tybalt was enraged, "This man I defy!
Now by the stock and honour of my kin,
To strike him dead, I hold it not a sin."
But across the room Lord Capulet strode.
He observed Tybalt's anger ready to explode.
"Calm yourself!" Capulet said in a low tone,
"You'll not spoil this party! Leave him alone!"
Tybalt cried, "This is a Montague, our foe!
'Tis he, that villain, Romeo!"
Capulet hissed, "Am I the master here, or you?
Stop this insolent behaviour. It will not do!"
"I will withdraw," Tybalt sneered with disdain,
"But this intrusion shall lead to pain!"

Put a sock in it Tybalt! It's a party. You should be merry! Romeo is not harming anyone. And who's in charge here anyway, you or me? I believe it is me SO JUST COOL IT!!!
Lord Capulet

Story: Elly Vousden (age 8)
Picture: Eliza Johnson (age 8)

Now Romeo heard none of this heated debate
For his thoughts of the lady would not abate.
His eyes locked with Juliet's across the room,
His identity hidden by a masked costume.
She was even more beautiful as he drew near,
And the warmth of her smile was sincere.
Her eyes grew bright; she felt total bliss,
Romeo took her hand and begged a kiss.
The lovers embraced, their hearts were set beating.
But the rapture they felt, alas, was fleeting.

Tonight at my father's party I met the most perfect gentleman. We gazed into each other's eyes for what seemed like forever. Then he gently kissed me. His kiss was warm and beautiful, soft as a daisy. My heart almost stopped completely. It was a heavenly experience!
Juliet

Story: Sarah Moore (age 7)
Picture: Eliza Johnson (age 8)

Juliet's nurse appeared from out of the blue,
"Madame, your mother craves a word with you."
Reluctantly, Juliet had to obey,
And with a backward glance she turned away.
"What is her mother?" Romeo inquired.
The nurse replied, "One much admired.
The lady of the house and a good woman, too!
Wise and virtuous, in my humble view."
Then the nurse turned and rushed away.
Romeo was stunned and filled with dismay,
"Oh dear account! My life is my foe's debt.
The girl I love is a Capulet!"
Soon Benvolio beckoned. It was time to leave,
"There's nothing more here we can achieve."

My one true love is my one true enemy. Cupid's arrow has missed but it was so close to a bull's eye. Oh if only she wasn't a Capulet! My love for her is stronger than any force in the universe. My life is crushed! Oh what will I do?
                                    Romeo

Lady Capulet

Story: Evan Ohler (age 7)
Picture: Elly Vousden (age 8)

19

Now Juliet, too, was in a trance,
"Who is that man who would not dance?"
She spoke to the nurse, "Don't let him go.
Ask his name. I need to know!
If he be married," Juliet said,
"My grave is like to be my wedding bed."
When she heard he was a Montague,
She couldn't believe that it was true,
"My only love sprung from my only hate,
Too early seen unknown and known too late.
Prodigious birth of love it is to me
That I must love a loathed enemy."
The nurse replied, "Anon, anon!
Come, let's away. The strangers all are gone."

Juliet

Dear Diary,
The most dreadful thing has happened! I adore my enemy young Romeo, a Montague! Pools of love trickled down my cheeks. I thought my heart would explode!!! Generations from now whoever reads this tear stained page of truth and love will weep for me!
Juliet

Story: Eliza Johnson (age 7)
Picture: Elly Vousden (age 8)

20

When Romeo left, he went on ahead.
His love for a Capulet filled him with dread.
"Can I go forward when my heart is here?"
He couldn't leave Juliet, that was clear.
He found himself near Capulet's wall.
In the distance, he heard Mercutio call,
"Romeo! Madman! Passion! Lover!"
Romeo scrambled over and quickly took cover.
He hid himself among the trees
As his friends drew near and continued to tease.
"I conjure thee by Rosaline's scarlet lip,"
Said Mercutio, unaware of the new courtship.
Benvolio tried to calm his comrade,
"Stop, Mercutio, you'll just make him mad."
"Romeo, good night!" Mercutio mockingly said.
Then in good spirits, they stumbled home to bed.

Elly Vousden (age 8)

Shrouded in darkness, Romeo looked around,
"My friend jests at scars," he sadly frowned.
"Those who mock love ne'er felt its aches.
But soft! What light through yonder window breaks?"
Romeo quivered. His heart took a leap.
His beloved Juliet was not asleep.
She stepped onto the balcony, into the night.
Romeo was entranced by this shining sight,
"It is the East and Juliet is the sun!
Her beauty cannot be outdone."

Oh me, oh my, it is the fair Juliet up on the balcony. Her brightness shatters the night and fills my heart with joy. She is a precious jewel in my life and the key to my soul. Oh my princess how I love thee! You are a perfect woman!

Story: Matthew Wilhelm (age 7)
Picture: Katie Hopkins (age 7)

Romeo

22

As Romeo watched from his hiding place,
To the stars above, Juliet stated her case,
"Oh Romeo, Romeo!" her eyes were aglow,
"Wherefore art thou Romeo?
'Tis but thy name that is my enemy.
Without the word, Montague, we would be free!
If that cannot be, my name I'll forget,
And I'll no longer be a Capulet!
Romeo, doff thy name which is no part of thee,
And for thy name take all of me."

23

Romeo proclaimed, "My name I disown!"
Juliet was amazed. She thought she was alone.
"Who are you veiled in the shadowy night,
Attending my secrets, out of sight?"
When she saw it was Romeo she felt dismay,
"Oh gentle Montague. You must leave right away!
If any of my kinsmen find thee here,
They will murder thee, that is clear."
Romeo answered, "I'm not afraid.
My love for you will never fade.
Juliet, please, you must give me a sign!
The exchange of thy love's faithful vow for mine!"

Oh Juliet, we are like two peas in a pod that soon must separate. Your name shivers through my brain. My mind burns for your love.
Romeo

Good Romeo, your message is exquisite but life is a poem and a poem is life. So be not wounded by my dreaded words. Romeo, I am afeared for your life. If you be true, stay but a little. My soul is locked in sorrow!
Juliet

Romeo

Story (top): David Marklevitz (age 8)
Story (bottom): Ellen Stuart (age 8)
Picture: Katie Besworth (age 8)

24

So under the shimmering stars above
Juliet gave her pledge of love,
"My bounty is as boundless as the sea.
My love as deep. The more I give to thee
The more I have, for both are infinite," she cried,
Her heart could no longer be denied.
"Send me word tomorrow!" Juliet said.
"Tell me where and when, we could be wed.
I believe your intentions to me are true.
Do not deceive me, sweet Montague.
Parting is such sweet sorrow
That I shall say good night till it be morrow."

Elly Vousden (age 8)

Now in a monastery, just out of town,
There lived a monk of considerable renown.
His habit was to rise at early hours
To collect his precious herbs and flowers.
These special plants held much appeal,
For they had the power to kill and to heal.
Friar Laurence was busy about this task,
When Romeo appeared, still carrying his mask.
"You're up mighty early!" the Friar said with zest.
"I do conclude your brain is not at rest.
Or if not so, then here I hit it right,
Our Romeo hath not been in bed tonight.
And now, my son, your confessions define.
Were you with the fair Rosaline?"

The Friar's Herb Garden

Rosemary — It helps headaches.

Thyme — It cures coughs and sore throats.

Parsley — It helps get rid of kidney stones.

Garlic — It treats ear infections.

Plantain — It cures poison ivy

Rue — It treats snake bites.

Sage — It fights colds and the flu.

Story: Gwyneth Schaeffer (age 8)
Picture: Valerie Sproat (age 10)

Friar Laurence

"With Rosaline, oh my dear father, no!
I have forgot that name, and that name's woe."
As the passionate story slowly unfolded,
The Friar listened and then gently scolded,
"Holy Saint Francis! What a change is here!
Is Rosaline, that thou didst love so dear,
So soon forsaken? Young men's love then lies,
Not truly in their hearts, but in their eyes.
But perhaps your marriage will be the key,
And to end the feuding, I will agree."

Teenagers! They're always acting so strange! Yesterday Romeo was mumbling and grumbling for Rosaline. Now he's weeping and wailing for another young lady. Who will it be next ... Queen Elizabeth? Just call me a confused Friar.

Friar Laurence

Romeo

Story: Brock Wreford (age 7)
Picture: Rebecca Courtney (age 8)

Back in Verona, Romeo's friends were perplexed.
After the feast, where had he gone next?
Benvolio was worried, "He stayed out all night!
And Tybalt has sent him a challenge to fight!"
Mercutio scoffed, "Romeo's already been slain.
That hard-hearted Rosaline has driven him insane."
But they needn't have worried, for lo and behold,
Down the road came the Romeo of old.
He matched wits with his friends, feeling upbeat,
Then Juliet's nurse bustled down the street.

Tybalt

A Challenge to Romeo

How dare you take one step
into Capulet's house. You are
a M-o-n-t-a-g-u-e! I won't
even say the dreadful name.
I challenge you to a contest
at quarter to 4pm in the
market square. I'm warning
you, against my anger you
don't stand a chance. Be
there or you'll be sorry!
        Your outraged enemy,
            Tybalt

Story: Sean McGarry (age 7)
Picture: Sydney Truelove (age 7)

"Gentlemen," she cried, as she dashed to and fro,
"Where may I find the young Romeo?
I'm instructed to talk with him alone!"
Romeo stepped forward and made himself known.
"This woman's a charmer!" Mercutio teased,
"Farewell, ancient lady!" The nurse wasn't pleased.
"What saucy merchant was this?" she retorted in shock.
"A gentleman," Romeo said, "that loves to hear himself talk.
But now, to Juliet, bid her come soon,
To the good Friar's cell this afternoon.
My servant will bring a rope ladder to you,
We'll use it tonight for our rendezvous.
Quickly, nurse, too long we have tarried,
At the Friar's, Juliet and I will be married."

Elly Vousden (age 8)

Meanwhile, Juliet was filled with concern,
"In half an hour, my nurse promised to return.
But three hours have passed since she went away!
Oh why does she not come back today?"
As Juliet paced and nervously waited,
The nurse finally appeared, all agitated,
"I am aweary. Fie, how my bones ache!
Let me sit down! Give me a break!"
Juliet cried, "But did you have your chat?
What says he of our marriage? What of that?"
"Juliet, I'm out of breath, can't you see?
Dear girl, you'll be the death of me.
But hasten now to the Friar's and a new life.
There stays a husband to make you a wife."

The Nurse

Oh my child, I am half dead from that errand you sent me on! I survived three hours of splitting headaches and back pains. He is a good lad, that Romeo is, as handsome as can be and twice as polite. Now run along child, your betrothed is waiting for you!

The Nurse

Story: Anika Johnson (age 8)
Picture: Ashley Kropf (age 10)

At the monk's cell, Romeo was elated.
He spoke with Laurence and impatiently waited.
The Friar prayed to the heavens above,
"Smile on this marriage and bless this love.
That after hours with sorrow, chide us not!"
For the Friar with gnawing doubts was fraught.
But when Juliet arrived and her love he beheld,
Laurence's worries were quickly dispelled,
"You shall not stay alone, my daughter and son
Till holy church incorporate two in one.
My children, we'll make this short and sweet."
And with the marriage, their bond was complete.

Elly Vousden (age 8)

31

Now back in the square in the heat of the day,
Benvolio was worried, "Come let's away!
There are too many Capulets roaming about!
We should leave this street, I have no doubt."
But Mercutio was begging for a fight
When hot-headed Tybalt came into sight.
The Capulet cried, "A word with my foe!"
Mercutio taunted, "Make it a word and a blow!"
Tybalt quickly lost interest in this affair
When he saw Romeo enter the square.
Tybalt thundered, "Here comes my man!"
And on that hot day, a new fight began.
But Romeo offered not a single threat,
"I hold dear to my heart, the name Capulet!"

Tybalt

A feeling of dread swept over me. A chill of fear ran down my spine. Sweat was resting on my brow. Mercutio is in the mood for another crushing blow. Then hot tempered Tybalt barged into the scene, his mighty blade swinging in the air. Verona is doomed once again!

A Worried citizen

Story: Brock Wreford (age 7)
Picture: Sydney Truelove (age 7)

Mercutio could not believe his ears.
He was inflamed by Tybalt's jeers,
"Romeo, a coward?" Mercutio was in shock.
"Tybalt, you rat catcher, will you walk?"
"What do you want of me?" Tybalt cried.
They glared at each other with insolent pride.
They crossed their swords without delay,
Then Romeo jumped into the fray,
"Gentlemen, for shame! Put an end to this fight!"
He seized his friend and held on tight.
Tybalt lunged at Mercutio with his blade.
Mercutio clutched at his chest and swayed,
"I am hurt!" he cried as Tybalt fled,
"A plague on both your houses! I am sped!"

Anika Johnson (age 8)

"A scratch, a scratch," Mercutio winced in pain.
His strength was now beginning to wane,
"Romeo! Why did you interfere?
He stabbed me under your arm right here.
Quick, Benvolio, give aid to my complaint.
Help me into some house or I shall faint."
In misery, Romeo stared after his friend,
"This is not what I did intend.
Mercutio did not have a fair shake.
He's been mortally wounded for my sake."
Benvolio reappeared, hanging his head,
"Oh Romeo, Romeo, brave Mercutio is dead!"

My head hangs low with sadness! All my happy thoughts are crushed into dust. Oh why did this happen to my dear friend Mercutio? He brought joy to my heart, laughter to my ear and now he's dead! There will never be another friend like him. May his soul rest in peace!

Romeo

Story: Eliza Johnson (age 7)
Picture: Sydney Truelove (age 7)

Romeo

Romeo felt anger as never before.
He despised Tybalt to the very core,
"Revenge for my lost friend I vow,
And fire-eyed fury be my conduct now!"
His wild rage he could no longer contain,
When Tybalt returned to fight once again.
Romeo lunged at him with a passionate leap,
And Tybalt fell to the ground in a heap.
Benvolio gasped under his breath,
"He's dead! The Prince will doom thee death."
"I am fortune's fool!" Romeo cried, "I'll retreat."
And he left Tybalt lying in the street.

Nothing grips my mind except revenge. Tybalt appeared proud and unfriendly, a sneering grin on his face. His eyes were like arrows and mine were as red as flames.

Romeo

Sean McGarry (age 7)

Jeremiah Courtney (age 10)

As Romeo hastily fled the square,
The Prince arrived to inspect the affair,
"Where are the vile beginners of this fray?"
Benvolio bowed low and was quick to obey,
"Oh noble Prince, I can discover all
The unlucky manage of this fatal brawl."
When Benvolio was finished he said with a sigh,
"This is the truth, or let Benvolio die!"
Lady Capulet was next, "As thou art true,
For blood of ours, shed blood of Montague!
I beg for justice, which thou, Prince, must give.
Romeo slew Tybalt; Romeo must not live!"

Anika Johnson (age 8)

The Prince interrupted; he was angry indeed,
"Neither man obeyed what I had decreed.
Romeo slew Tybalt, who'd slain Mercutio.
Who shall pay the price of that fatal blow?"
Lord Montague listened and then spoke at the end,
"Not Romeo, Prince, he was Mercutio's friend;
He took Tybalt's life, good Prince, that is true,
But he only did what the law would do."
The Prince commanded, "And for that offence
Immediately we do exile him hence.
Never again shall we see Romeo's face,
For he will die if he returns to this place.
Bear hence this body, and attend our will.
Mercy but murders, pardoning those that kill."

I've been put in a terrible situation. What should I do about Romeo Montague? I understand the grief Romeo feels. He has lost a best friend. But he should have come to me with the problem. Now it's too late and the law is the law. I declare that Romeo shall be BANISHED never to return.
          Prince Escalus

Story and picture: Katie Besworth (age 8)

Prince Escalus

Now, Juliet knew nothing of the terrible fight.
She paced in her room, awaiting the night.
Each hour to her seemed terribly long.
Then the nurse arrived, but something was wrong.
She was wringing her hands and stared straight ahead,
"Alack the day! He's gone, he's killed, he's dead!
We are undone, lady. How could we know?
Who ever would have thought it? Romeo!"
"Hath Romeo slain himself?" Juliet grew tense,
"Oh nurse, don't keep me in suspense!"
"Oh Tybalt, Tybalt!" The nurse hung her head,
"That ever I should live to see thee dead!"
Juliet cried, "You mean both are gone?
Who is left living so I can carry on?"

Dear Diary,
Who is left to love me?
My heart is split in two
like a coconut. My tears
stream down my cheeks
like a monsoon in the
jungle. Oh why is it me
who wallows in sorrow?
My heart is lost in the
darkness, without a light
to guide my way.
          Juliet

Story: Brock Wreford (age 7)
Picture: Ashley Kropf (age 10)

The Nurse

"Romeo killed Tybalt!" the nurse sounded wild,
"Tybalt is gone and Romeo exiled!"
Juliet's eyes grew wide; she felt her heart thud,
"Did Romeo's hand shed Tybalt's blood?
Oh serpent heart, hid with a flowering face!
Are you sure, good nurse, this is the case?"
The nurse cursed, "Shame come to Romeo!
There's no honesty in men, you know."
Tears filled Juliet's eyes to the brim,
"Oh, what a beast was I to chide at him!
Romeo was not born to shame.
My husband should not take the blame!"
The nurse relented, "He's at Laurence's cell.
I'll tell him to come for his last farewell."
Juliet smiled, "Give him my ring.
This evening will my true love bring."

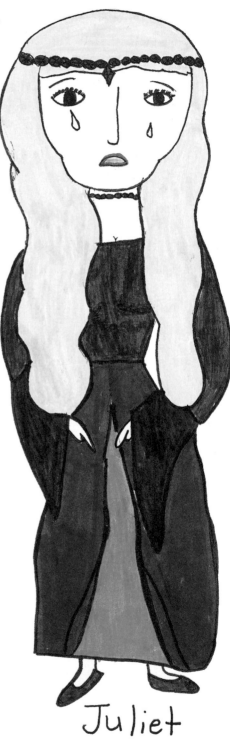

Juliet

I should have a face as bright as a rainbow and a heart glowing with joy. But my dreams are demolished. I am locked in a tale of destroyed lives. To find the key is the biggest mystery of all.
Juliet

Story: Josh Strasler (age 7)
Picture: Eliza Johnson (age 8)

39

As Romeo waited to hear of his doom,
He paced back and forth in the Friar's room.
"Good Friar, tell me what is the decree?
What sentence has been pronounced on me?"
The Friar declared, "The Prince is content,
Not with your death, but with banishment."
"Banishment?" Romeo wailed, "Save your breath."
He fell to the ground, "Be merciful, say death!"
The Friar replied, "Don't be so distraught.
This is dear mercy, and thou see'st it not."
At that moment there was a loud knock,
"Quick Romeo, hide!" Laurence begged in shock.
"Run to my study! Good Romeo arise!
You will be taken! It will be your demise!"

Romeo

Banished!
What did you say?

The word makes me humble
My hands start to fumble
My heart starts to tumble
The fog of despair.

My legs start to weave
My chest starts to heave
Juliet I must leave
The fog of despair.

Story: Ellen Stuart (age 9)
Picture: Megan Vandersleen (age 9)

But it was the nurse who stood at the door.
"I have a message you cannot ignore.
Where's Juliet's husband?" she asked the monk.
"There on the ground, with his own tears made drunk!"
"My mistress," she said, "is as wretched as he,
Blubbering and weeping, even so lies she.
A word with you Romeo, I demand.
For Juliet's sake, for her sake, rise and stand!"
Romeo obeyed, "How is it with her?
Doth not she think me an old murderer?"
He drew his sword, overcome by woe,
"I'll deal myself a mortal blow!"

The Nurse

Oh, what a child Romeo has turned into. For shame I say, for shame! I am getting a little fed up with this Romeo business! He thinks exile is worse than death! He is putting too much weight on love and not enough on life! As I always say, too much weight leaves too little!
                    The Nurse

Story and picture: Elly Vousden (age 8)

41

The Friar shouted, "Hold thy desperate hand,
I am amazed by your frantic stand.
Go to your wife. Let nothing impede.
Ascend her chamber, as was agreed,
But leave Verona by morn's early light.
Disguise yourself and stay out of sight.
In Mantua, you will abide alone,
Till we can make your marriage known.
Both of your families, I'll try to convince,
And I will beg pardon of the Prince."
The nurse gave Romeo the ring from his mate,
"Make haste," she said, "for it grows very late!"

Dear Romeo,
What is this madness? One moment you are weeping about banishment and the next you are trying to end your life. What is wrong with you boy? Your behaviour is atrocious! Hasten to Juliet and comfort her. You need to cope now. Time is running out.
                    Friar Laurence

Story: Eliza Johnson (age 7)
Picture: Michelle Stevenson (age 11)

Friar Laurence

Back at Juliet's, her father was distressed,
"I hate to see my daughter so depressed.
I know she loved Tybalt with all her soul,
But her weeping is completely out of control."
He spoke with Count Paris, "to your suit I agree.
I believe Juliet will be guided by me.
We'll cheer her up. I know just what to do.
In a few days she'll be married to you.
We'll plan for it Wednesday!" Capulet said,
"No, that's too soon, make it Thursday instead."
Paris was joyful, "It will end her sorrow.
My lord, I would that Thursday were tomorrow!"

Dear Paris,
Oh how Juliet weeps
in sorrow. Tybalt was
a good friend to her.
But we all have a time
of birth and death. It's
the way of the world.
I must put a stop to
this moaning. Being a
father can be very
difficult.
             Lord Capulet

Story: Piers Fox (age 7)
Picture: Katie Hopkins (age 7)

Lord Capulet

43

Now Juliet was locked in Romeo's arms,
In a blessed night of enchanted charms.
The unwanted dawn came much too soon.
The lark seemed to trill a displeasing tune.
"It is not yet near day!" Juliet turned pale.
"Believe me, love, it was the nightingale."
Now Romeo spoke, just as forlorn,
"It was the lark, the herald of the morn.
Though this day's dawning we wish to deny,
I must be gone and live, or stay and die!"
Juliet sighed, "More light and light it grows."
Romeo added, "More dark and dark our woes."

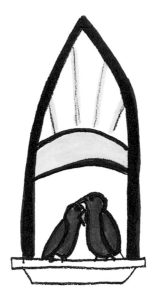

Top: Shannon Campbell (age 9)
Bottom: Elly Vousden (age 8)

44

The nurse appeared, "Your mother's coming out.
The day is broke. Be wary. Look about."
In a final moment of wedded bliss,
The lovers embraced for one last kiss.
Then Romeo descended to the ground,
And disappeared without a sound.
Reluctantly, Juliet turned away.
Her mother appeared, "How are you today?
Evermore weeping for Tybalt's death?
I've happy news!" she said in the next breath.
"The noble Count Paris," she spoke with pride,
"On Thursday shall make thee a joyful bride."
"Never!" Juliet shouted, "I will not marry yet!"
Then into the room strode Lord Capulet.

> Dear Mother,
> I beg of you do not make me marry Count Paris. He is the very despair of my heart. We would never get along. Besides, I do not love him. His riches mean nothing to me. He is not the key to my soul.
> Your Pleading Daughter,
> Juliet

Théa Pel (age 7)

Eliza Johnson (age 8)

"Good wife, have you told our daughter the plan?"
"I have, my lord. She refuses the man."
Capulet glared at his daughter, "You will obey!
My word to Paris I won't betray.
To St. Peter's Church! Find you the course,
Or I will drag you there by force."
Juliet wailed, "I beseech you on my knees.
Hear me with patience, if you please."
"Speak not!" he replied, "For I do not jest!
Till you marry the Count, I will not rest.
Or hang, beg, starve, die in the street!"
And with that her father made a hasty retreat.

You listen to me young Lady! If you do not marry Paris, you will never lay foot in this house again! And don't you "but daddy" me! This man loves you and you won't even give him a crumb of your heart. Your conduct is appalling!
Lord Capulet

Lord Capulet

Story: Tibby Leushius (age 8)
Picture: Katie Hopkins (age 7)

46

"Oh, sweet my mother, cast me not away!
This marriage you must try to delay!"
Lady Capulet scoffed, "Talk not to me.
Do as thou wilt, for I have done with thee!"
Juliet despaired, "I must think of a ploy.
Good nurse, hast thou not a word of joy?"
The nurse encouraged, "The Count is a fine catch!
I know you'll be happy in this second match."
"Speakest thou from thy heart?" Juliet cried.
"And from my soul, too!" the nurse replied.
Even her servant had proved untrue.
Juliet thought of the Friar, "He'll know what to do!"

Dear Juliet,
You are in major trouble. I expected much more from you. I thought you were a child with some sense in you but I see that I am wrong. I shall have no more to do with you.
Your Mother,
Lady Capulet

Story: Andrea Petrak (age 7)
Picture: Ashley Kropf (age 10)

But Friar Laurence already had a guest.
Count Paris was there with his marriage request.
He longed to begin his wedded life.
Then he saw Juliet, "My lady and my wife!
In just a few days you'll be married to me."
Juliet replied, "What must be shall be."
Count Paris noticed nothing amiss,
"Till then, adieu, and keep this holy kiss!"
Then from the monastery Paris sped.
Juliet's heart was filled with dread.
"Good Friar," she sobbed, "Come weep with me.
Past hope, past cure, past help you see.
If you can't give me remedy, I'll end my life.
Behold, I'll do it with this knife!"

Juliet

Oh holy pastor, join me in my pools of sorrow. Help free me from this cage of despair. My life and love are both banished with my husband to Mantua. And to have two husbands—Now that would be a tragedy. Respond to me at once or my knife shall make the choice!

Juliet

Story: Matthew Wilhelm (age 7)
Picture: Rebecca Courtney (age 8)

48

"Wait, my child, there's a glimmer of hope.
I have a plan but it's desperate in scope.
Before you decide or give your consent,
Listen and I will describe each event.
Go home, be merry, in your parents confide.
Tell them you will be Count Paris's bride.
Then tomorrow night when no one is there,
Drink from this vial a potion most rare.
Your blood will soon chill and you will feel weak,
Your eyelids will droop, and you shall not speak.
The roses in your lips and cheeks shall fade,
No warmth, no breath, no pulse will be displayed.

Théa Pel (age 8)

"This likeness of death from the potion's powers
Shall continue to work for many hours.
When your parents find you in your bed,
They will believe that you are dead.
In Capulet's tomb your body will be laid.
I'll send word to Romeo about the charade.
Then out of this deathlike slumber deep,
You will awaken as from a sweet sleep.
Your Romeo and I will both be there;
And he'll take you to Mantua in his care."
Juliet's face grew flushed, "I will do the deed.
Love will give me the strength to succeed."

Juliet

Friar Laurence's Plan

① Run home with a smile as bright as a sunflower. Agree to marry the Count.

② Go directly to your room. Make sure not a soul peeks in.

③ Drink the potion. Don't worry when your teeth shiver and a weak chill floods your body.

④ You will be taken to the tomb and rest for 42 hours.

⑤ I will notify Romeo. We will be there when you awake.

Story: Josh Strasler (age 7)
Picture: Katie Hopkins (age 7)

Juliet rushed home with hopeful belief.
Her father greeted the change with relief.
"I'm glad my wishes you've decided to heed.
Send for the Count! This is great news indeed!
We'll not wait for Thursday! Begin her adorning.
I'll have this knot knit up tomorrow morning."
Then to her bedroom, Juliet quickly withdrew
To advance the Friar's plan, step two.
"Gentle nurse," she advised in a manner polite,
"I pray thee leave me to myself tonight."
But now her courage began to wane.
Horror and panic filled her brain.

As I left the Friar's the golden sun gleamed in the fresh morning mist. The trees swayed back and forth to the music of the moaning wind. As rain greeted the land its steady rhythm matched the beats of my heart.

Juliet

Story: Katie Besworth (age 8)
Picture: Sophie Jones (age 9)

Lord Capulet

Juliet's flesh began to crawl,
"What if this mixture does not work at all?
Then in the morning, I'll be forced to wed."
She laid a dagger beside the bed.
"This shall forbid it. It will stay by my side."
She picked up the potion, "What if the monk lied?
Suppose this is poison and the Friar's a fake?
Oh, could this all be a dreadful mistake?
And what if Romeo is late at the tomb?
I'd be left alone in that foul room!
Oh Romeo, Romeo, you hold the key!"
She lifted the vial, "I drink to thee!"

Chills of fear trickle past my wildly beating heart. My throat seems to tighten and my lungs feel pinched together. I can hardly breathe. I clutch the potion and drink the liquid. I feel my body sinking low into the mist. My conscience is falling into the forbidden circle of life......
Juliet

Story: Katie Besworth (age 8)
Picture: Elly Vousden (age 8)

At the crack of dawn, the excitement grew.
Count Paris arrived with his retinue.
Capulet called to the nurse, "Make haste, I say,
Go waken Juliet for her wedding day."
The nurse entered the chamber, "Get up!" she cried.
"Why, lamb! Why, lady! Why, love! Why, bride!
Dressed and in your clothes and now back in bed?"
The nurse turned pale, "Help! Help! My lady's dead!"
Juliet's mother was standing nearby.
She rushed into the room when she heard the outcry,
"Oh me, oh me! My child, my only life!"
Then Capulet strode in, "What's the matter, wife?"
"Alack!" she lamented, "Your daughter, behold!"
When he touched Juliet's body, she was cold.

My little lady, morning has come. It is time for the most blessed day of your life. Get up! The hour grows thin and your groom awaits. Oh lazy daisy! How deep a sleep can you be in?

The Nurse

Ellen Stuart (age 8)

Anika Johnson (age 8)

Then the Friar, with Paris, appeared below,
"Tell me, is the bride ready to go?"
Lord Capulet spoke low, his voice shook with concern,
"Ready to go, but never to return!
Count Paris, death has taken your wife.
Death is my son-in-law. Death take my life!"
But the Friar felt no grief in his heart.
Soon, Romeo and Juliet would have a fresh start.
By his friend, Friar John, the message had been sent,
Explaining to Romeo, each strange event.
Friar Laurence beseeched, "Dry up your tears!
Wash away all of your earthly fears!
And as the custom is, in her best array,
Bear Juliet to the church today!"

Oh heavenly glory! WHY did you take the life of my only daughter? I am crushed by the thought of it !!! Oh horrible sight. The impact of death has crawled up her heart. It pumps no more.

Lord Capulet

Story: David Marklevilz (age 8)
Picture: Kimberly Brown (age 11)

54

Romeo

In Mantua, Romeo knew none of this.
He dreamed of his loved one and future bliss.
He laughed aloud and was full of good cheer,
When Balthasar, his loyal servant, drew near.
"How now, my good friend, I must inquire,
Did you bring a letter from the Friar?
And how is my lady? Oh pray do tell
For nothing can be ill if she be well!"
"Forgive me, my lord, I bring tidings of doom,
Juliet's body lies in Capulet's tomb."
Romeo staggered, "Are you sure this is so?"
Balthasar answered,"I saw her, Romeo."
Romeo howled, "I defy my fate!
Hire the horses; I'll be with thee straight."

My loved one gone? Dead?
The words burn my heart.
She was more precious to
me than life itself. This
is the bitter end. All hope
is lost. The last rose has
wilted, the last leaf has
fallen and my candle has
burnt out. My fair Juliet,
I will be with you tonight!
Romeo

Sophie Jones (age 9)

Morgan Pel (age 8)

Romeo stood on the street all alone,
His hopes for the future now overthrown,
"Well Juliet, I will lie with thee tonight!
But I need the means to make it right."
He hastened to an apothecary,
To obtain the drugs that were necessary.
"Here's forty ducats!" Romeo cried.
"A dram of poison, you must provide!"
The apothecary muttered under his breath,
"To sell mortal drugs is punishable by death!
My poverty but not my will consents."
He offered the drug, "Its powers are intense."
Romeo clutched the drink, "You're not poison to me.
To Juliet's grave. For there must I use thee!"

To day a strange man came to my doorstep. He demanded a bottle of poison for forty ducats. My shop is in need of repair, my shingles must be replaced and my clothes are rags. I need those gold coins!
          A poor druggist

The Apothecary

Story: Sean McGarry (age 7)
Picture: Katie Besworth (age 8)

Now Friar Laurence was becoming frustrated,
And back in his room, he impatiently waited.
Finally, Friar John arrived at his cell.
"Welcome, dear brother. I hope all is well!"
But what Laurence heard next gave him a chill.
Friar John could not his orders fulfil,
"You see, Laurence, I never left this town.
I was visiting the sick," John said with a frown,
"When city officials sealed up the gate.
They suspected the plague. There was no debate!"
"Unhappy fortune!" Laurence cried in alarm,
"Bring me a crowbar. I fear some harm.
I will to the vault and enter the room.
Poor living corpse, closed in a dead man's tomb!"

Friar John

Friar Laurence

Jamie Foley (age 10)

Valerie Sproat (age 10)

But already there was another on guard
At the Capulets' vault in the lonely churchyard.
Young Paris wept as he stood alone,
"My Juliet's covered with dust and stone.
Sweet flowers I will lay on her bed,
And water them with the tears I shed."
Then he heard his page whistle, "I will hide here."
For this was their signal an intruder was near.
"Give me the torch!" It was Romeo's voice.
"Balthasar, stand away. You have no choice."
Then Romeo pried open the door to the tomb,
And prepared to descend into the room.

Ashley Kropf (age 10)

"Stop vile Montague!" The Count drew his sword.
"Leave me alone!" Romeo implored.
But Romeo's warning was in vain.
Their swords clashed in fury, and Paris was slain.
"It's Mercutio's kinsman," Romeo said with regret,
"I will bury him with my dear Juliet.
Gently he carried the body inside.
Then he knelt by his beloved wife and cried,
"Oh my love, my wife, why art thou yet so fair?"
Her beauty was more than he could bear.
"Death's pale colour has not yet touched your face."
He held her close in a final embrace.
Romeo found the poison and held it high,
"Here's to my love. Thus with a kiss I die!"

Romeo

There you lie, a thing of beauty,
no longer free to live and draw
breath. Oh my love, why must
you rest here dead, cold and limp?
Life is a never ending tragedy,
nothing but an ocean of sorrow,
ebbing and flowing. A tidal wave
of grief washes over me. One
last kiss and I shall join you
in your heavenly home.
                                    Romeo

Story: Anika Johnson (age 8)
Picture: Katie Besworth (age 8)

59

'Twas then the old Friar limped into the tomb.
Juliet would soon awake in the room.
But Laurence had seen the blood at the gate,
And he knew in his heart that it was too late.
He saw Romeo lying in a heap
As Juliet stirred from her lengthy sleep.
"Oh comfortable Friar. Where is my lord?
Where is my Romeo?" she implored.
"Come, come away!" he cried in remorse.
"Our plans are thwarted by a higher force.
Your husband lies dead and Paris, too!
I hear some noise. Oh what shall we do?
The watch is coming! I dare no longer stay!"
"Get thee hence," cried Juliet, "for I will not away!"

Dear Friar,
No, I shall not go with you. My heart has chosen my path and it is here with Romeo. The bondage of grief wraps me up in a tight knot. The invisible chain of love links us together and will never be unlocked.

Juliet

Brock Wreford (age 7)

Anika Johnson (age 8)

The Friar left her in the tomb below,
And she knelt one last time by her Romeo.
"What's here? A cup, closed in my true love's hand?
Poison, my lord! This is not what we planned!"
She drank from the bottle but it was dry,
"One friendly drop to me you deny?
I will kiss thy lips, some may remain there.
Thy lips are warm!" she moaned in despair.
"I hear them coming! The watchmen advance!"
She seized Romeo's dagger, "This is my last chance!"
Juliet stabbed herself, and life defied,
Then fell to the ground by Romeo's side.

Oh dearest love
pale like snow
blood no longer rushing
breath no longer flowing
there he lies
Oh Romeo speak comfort to me
I flood my tears into an ocean
so big so deep
that no living thing could survive
helpful dagger
steal my life
from this world of grief
life is worthless without thee.
                    Juliet

Story: Laura Bates (age 7)
Picture: Erin Patterson (age 10)

61

Both families arrived at this sad scene,
But it was too late to intervene.
Before the Prince, they knelt in grief.
Their children's lives had been much too brief.
Prince Escalus stood solemn in the tomb.
His voice of reason shattered the gloom,
"See what a scourge is laid upon your hate.
Your beloved ones gone in an act of fate.
And I for winking at your discords too
Have lost a brace of kinsmen true."
Finally, the families saw they were wrong,
And settled the feud after far too long.
And Lord Capulet and Lord Montague
Clasped hands in peace that was much overdue.

Lord Capulet

Lord Montague

Elly Vousden (age 8)

Statues of the lovers were raised out of gold,
So that all could remember and behold.
For never was a story of more woe,
Than this of Juliet and her Romeo.

Anika Johnson (age 9)

Parents and Educators

This book can be used for a variety of activities, either at home or in the classroom. Here are a few suggestions you might find helpful:

- Locate Verona, Italy, on a map of the world.

- Draw a street map of Verona, showing where the characters might have lived.

- Write a diary for Romeo or Juliet, adding to it daily.

- Design and construct masks and prepare entertainment (music and dance) for the Capulet ball.

- Dramatize the party, adding your own dialogue.

- Create a tableau (a "frozen picture") of a particular scene.

- Brainstorm all the similarities between the Montagues and the Capulets.

- Write a newspaper account of the wedding of Romeo and Juliet, the death of Mercutio, and the banishment of Romeo.

- List all the fight scenes in the play. Dramatize conflict resolution techniques, showing how the arguments could have been avoided.

- Post a Shakespearean Quote of the Day

- Plant some herbs that Friar Laurence might have grown in his garden. Find out about their uses.

Robin Wilhelm

Katie Besworth (age 8)

Educators who wish to stage performances of *Romeo and Juliet for Kids* should contact the author to request permission:
      Fax: (519) 273-0712
      E-mail: lburdett@orc.ca

Special thanks to Ann Stuart for her assistance and support.

Front cover and title page: Anika Johnson (age 8)
Back cover: David Marklevitz (age 8), Mackenzie Donaldson (age 8)